EARTH'S MOST EXTREME PLACES

EARTH'S HIGHEST PLACES

BY MARY GRIFFIN

Gareth Stevens
PUBLISHING

Please visit our website, www.garethstevens.com. For a free color catalog of all our high-quality books, call toll free 1-800-542-2595 or fax 1-877-542-2596.

Library of Congress Cataloging-in-Publication Data

Griffin, Mary, 1978- author.
Earth's highest places / Mary Griffin.
pages cm. — (Earth's most extreme places)
Includes index.
ISBN 978-1-4824-1898-9 (pbk.)
ISBN 978-1-4824-1897-2 (6 pack)
ISBN 978-1-4824-1899-6 (library binding)
1. Physical geography—Juvenile literature. 2. Altitudes—Juvenile literature. 3. Extreme environments—Juvenile literature. I. Title.
GB58.G75 2015
910'.02143—dc23

2014021954

First Edition

Published in 2015 by
Gareth Stevens Publishing
111 East 14th Street, Suite 349
New York, NY 10003

Designer: Katelyn E. Reynolds
Editor: Therese Shea

Photo credits: Cover, p. 1 Papa Lima Whiskey 2/Wikipedia.com; cover, pp. 1–24 (background texture) Adisa/Shutterstock.com; p. 5 (inset) Paula Bronstein/Getty Images; p. 5 (map) Sven Manguard/Wikipedia.com; p. 7 © iStockphoto.com/JoyfulThailand; pp. 9, 11 (map) Stannered/Wikipedia.com; p. 9 (main) Johnny Haglund/Lonely Planet Images/Getty Images; p. 11 (main) Dr. Morley Read/Shutterstock.com; p. 12 Alexey Kamenskiy/Shutterstock.com; p. 13 (map) NordNordWest/Wikipedia.com; p. 13 (main) Karin Wassmer/Shutterstock.com; p. 15 (inset diagram) Dorling Kindersley/Thinkstock.com; p. 15 (main) pcruciatti/Shutterstock.com; p. 17 (map) Haha169/Wikipedia.com; p. 17 (main) Irina Schmidt/Shutterstock.com; p. 18 robert paul van beets/Shutterstock.com; p. 19 Steve Heap/Shutterstock.com; p. 21 (mountain illustrations) Kozoriz Yuriy/Shutterstock.com; p. 21 (building illustrations) Dan/FreeVector.com; p. 21 (photo) Sean Pavone/Shutterstock.com.

Printed in the United States of America

CPSIA compliance information: Batch #CW15GS: For further information contact Gareth Stevens, New York, New York at 1-800-542-2595.

CONTENTS

Words in the glossary appear in **bold** type the first time they are used in the text.

MOUNT EVEREST

Mount Everest is famous for its height. It's the tallest mountain in the world at 29,035 feet (8,850 m) above sea level. Mount Everest is located between Nepal and Tibet in Asia. It's part of the Himalayas, a mountain range with many tall **peaks**.

Mount Everest is so high that mountain climbers couldn't reach the top until 1953. That year, Edmund Hillary and Tenzing Norgay were the first to do so. They had to avoid sheer drops, slick ice, deadly rocks, powerful winds, and freezing conditions to get there.

THAT'S EXTREME!

The Himalayas contain more than 110 mountains taller than 24,000 feet (7,315 m).

Many climbers have followed in Edmund Hillary and Tenzing Norgay's footsteps. Many have died trying.

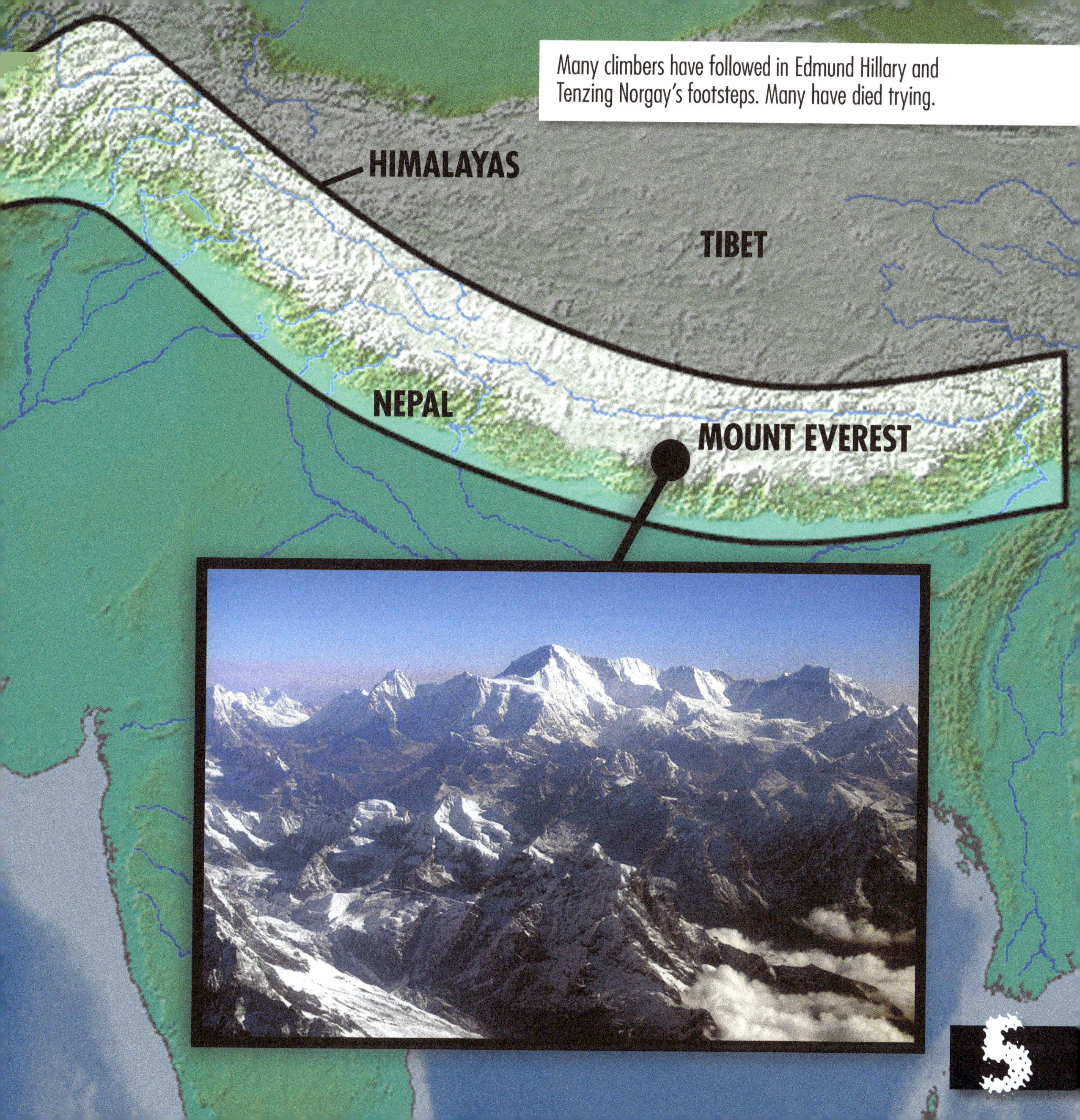

DANGER AT HIGH ALTITUDE

Another danger of being on top of Mount Everest—and other high peaks—is that there's less **oxygen** so high up in Earth's **atmosphere**. There's about one-third less oxygen than we breathe at sea level.

Low oxygen levels can cause dizziness or worse. **Altitude** sickness may lead to brain swelling, blackouts, and more. Most mountain climbers use bottled oxygen and masks so they can breathe more easily and avoid altitude sickness. They need to be at their best to avoid accidents, so extra oxygen is a smart idea.

THAT'S EXTREME!

Moving back down a mountain may help altitude sickness, but it can turn deadly if a climber isn't treated or moved fast enough.

Your body needs a certain amount of oxygen in the air to function well.

HIGHEST CITY

People manage to live in some very high places. The magazine *National Geographic* gives the title of highest city in the world to La Rinconada, Peru, which is found at 16,732 feet (5,100 m) above sea level. It's a tough place to live. Temperatures are freezing so high up. There isn't running water or a system of transporting waste away from the city.

More than 30,000 people live there to work in nearby mines, searching for gold. Sometimes, as extra payment, miners are allowed to carry home whatever they can find for themselves.

THAT'S EXTREME!

The highest town in the United States is Alma, Colorado, at about 10,578 feet (3,224 m).

The people of La Rinconada are very poor, which is why they live in such harsh conditions. They hope to make enough money to support their families.

MOUNT CHIMBORAZO

Mount Everest is the highest mountain from sea level to peak. However, it isn't the highest point on Earth. How can this be true?

Earth isn't a perfect **sphere**. It's shaped a bit like a flattened ball. That means that a part of it **bulges** out a bit more. A mountain sitting on the highest part of that bulge—Mount Chimborazo in Ecuador—is thought to be the highest point on Earth. Measuring from the center of Earth, Mount Chimborazo is taller than Mount Everest by about 1.5 miles (2.4 km).

Mount Chimborazo is found in the Andes mountain range. It's 20,702 feet (6,310 m) above sea level.

MAUNA KEA

There's another mountain taller than Mount Everest. It's called Mauna Kea (MOW-nah KAY-ah), and it's in Hawaii. It rises 33,484 feet (10,206 m) from base to peak. It's not said to be the tallest mountain on Earth because its base is below sea level. People only see about 13,796 feet (4,205 m) of the mountain rising above the ocean.

The peak is the site of the Mauna Kea **Observatory**. Some of the best telescopes are located there because the conditions to view space from atop the mountain are so good.

Most of the time, the skies above Mauna Kea are clear. When there are clouds, the peak is usually above the clouds.

BUILDING MOUNTAINS

Many mountains form when the pieces that make up Earth's crust, called tectonic plates, push against each other. The force causes the matter that makes up the plates to crumple, pushing up and creating mountain ranges like the Himalayas. This process happens over millions of years and is still happening.

Other mountains are formed when hot **magma** beneath Earth's surface **erupts**. This is called a volcano. **Lava**, ash, and rock cool and can pile up into a mountain. Mauna Kea and Mount Chimborazo are both volcanoes.

THAT'S EXTREME!

When two of Earth's plates slip past each other, an earthquake occurs.

Sometimes it's easy to see where two of Earth's plates are crashing into each other.

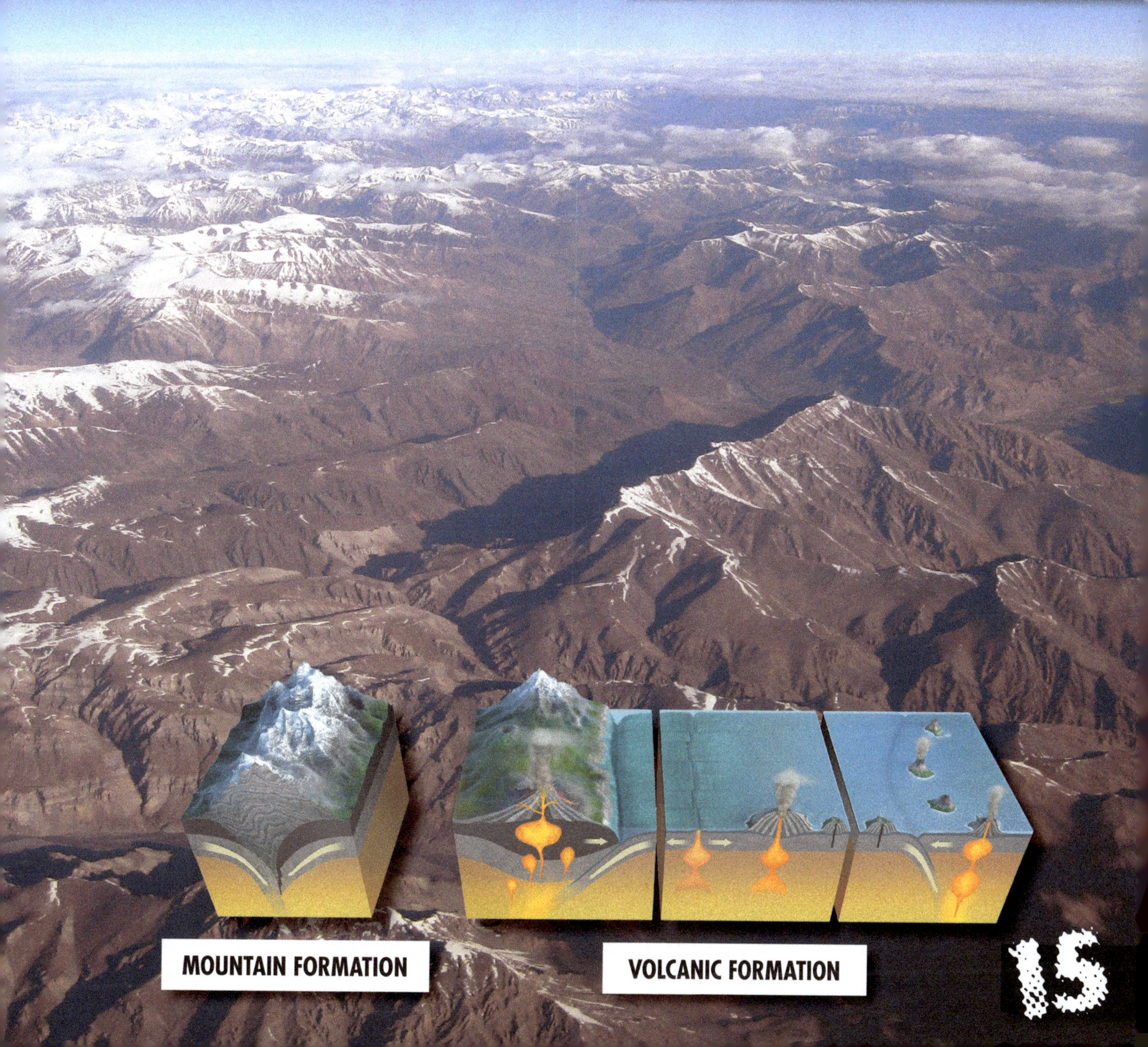

MOUNTAIN FORMATION

VOLCANIC FORMATION

BURJ KHALIFA

Mountains aren't the only high places on Earth. People build very tall **structures**. Though none are as tall as the mountains in this book, they're still extremely tall. The tallest building in the world is called Burj Khalifa, which means "Khalifa Tower." It's located in Dubai in the United Arab Emirates.

The builders kept the planned height a secret while construction went on. When it was completed in 2010, Burj Khalifa was 2,717 feet (828 m) tall. It has 162 floors and is used for businesses and apartments.

THAT'S EXTREME!

Burj Khalifa easily beat the previous tallest building, the Taipei 101 (Taipei Financial Center) building in Taipei, Taiwan. It's 1,667 feet (508 m) tall.

People can walk out onto a deck on the 124th floor of Burj Khalifa.

ONE WORLD TRADE CENTER

When One World Trade Center in New York City was completed in 2013, it became the tallest building in the Western **Hemisphere**. It towers at 1,776 feet (541 m). The glass and steel sides are meant to reflect back the colors of the sky and city lights around it.

One World Trade Center is built on the site of the old World Trade Center. The twin towers of the World Trade Center (right) were attacked and destroyed by **terrorists** on September 11, 2001. The new building is a sign of hope for a peaceful future.

The new One World Trade Center includes a memorial to the people whose lives were lost in the terrorist attack.

ALWAYS HIGHER

There are many other very tall buildings in the United States and around the world. However, many of the tallest man-made structures are towers built to send TV and radio signals. People are always trying to build stronger, taller structures.

In 2014, it was announced that a building called Kingdom Tower would be built in Saudi Arabia. It's planned to be an amazing 3,280 feet (1 km) tall. Will they succeed in building the new tallest building in the world?

THAT'S EXTREME!

Building the Kingdom Tower will require about 5.7 million square feet (530,000 sq m) of concrete and 80,000 tons (72,560 mt) of steel.

HOW HIGH?

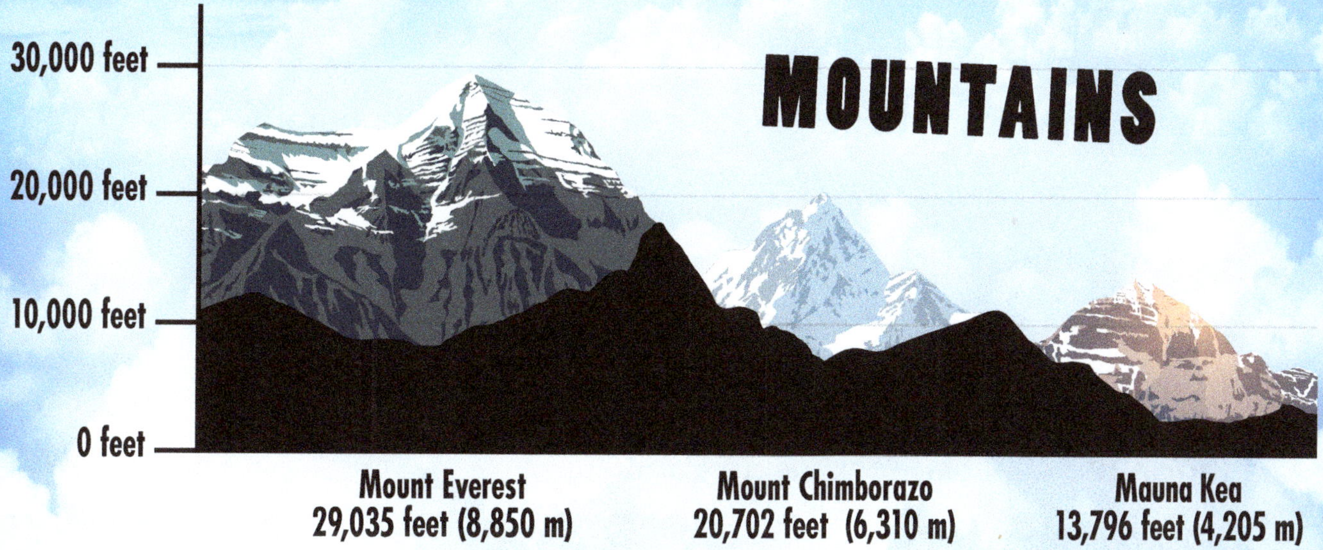

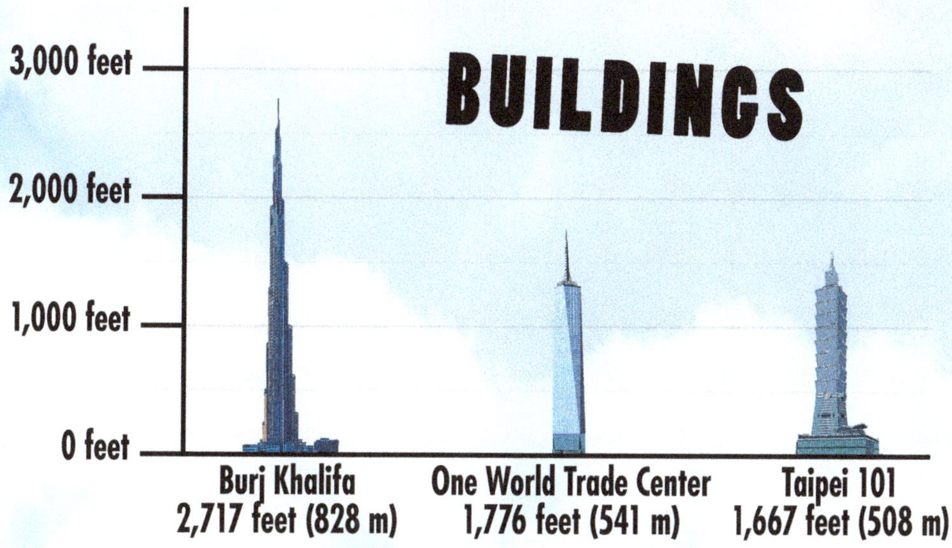

Taipei 101, Taiwan

GLOSSARY

altitude: height above sea level

atmosphere: the mixture of gases that surround a planet

bulge: to expand or swell

erupt: to burst forth

hemisphere: one-half of Earth

lava: hot, liquid rock that comes out of a volcano

magma: hot, liquid rock inside Earth

observatory: a place used for the scientific observation of heavenly bodies

oxygen: a colorless, odorless gas that many animals, including people, need to breathe

peak: the pointed top of a mountain

sphere: an object shaped like a ball

structure: an object such as a bridge or building that has been put together from many parts

terrorist: one who uses violence and fear to challenge an authority

FOR MORE INFORMATION

BOOKS

Dickmann, Nancy. *Mount Everest.* Chicago, IL: Raintree, 2012.

Gilpin, Daniel. *Record-Breaking Buildings.* New York, NY: PowerKids Press, 2012.

Rustad, Martha E. H. *The Highest Places on Earth.* Mankato, MN: Capstone Press, 2010.

WEBSITES

Earth Science Records
geology.com/records/
Find out more record-breaking facts on this site.

How Mountains Are Formed
www.universetoday.com/29833/how-mountains-are-formed/
Read more about how mountains are formed.

Publisher's note to educators and parents: Our editors have carefully reviewed these websites to ensure that they are suitable for students. Many websites change frequently, however, and we cannot guarantee that a site's future contents will continue to meet our high standards of quality and educational value. Be advised that students should be closely supervised whenever they access the Internet.

INDEX